GW00467734

PAIDEIA EDUCATION

JOHN STEINBECK

The Grapes of Wrath

Literary analysis

Paideia Education

© Paideia Education, 2020.

ISBN 978-2-7593-0706-7

Legal Deposit: september 2020

Printing Books on Demand GmbH

In de Tarpen 42

22848 Norderstedt, Germany

CONTENTS

AUTHOR'S
BIOGRAPHY

John Steinbeck is an American author who was born in Salinas, California, in 1902, and who died of a heart attack in New York in 1968. He received the Nobel Price of literature and his literary work is one of the most important in the American cultural history. He was often described as a man with the vigorous constitution of his German ancestors combined with a good sense of humour, and with a taste for mystery and for the poetic values inherited from his Irish ascendency. *Of Mice And Men* (1937), *The Grapes of Wrath* (1939), and *East of Eden* (1949) are his best known literary works both in his country and abroad.

He was the son of a lawyer and a teacher and grew up in a city where cowboys organized great rodeos; the young Steinbeck was blown away and mistreated by life at an early age.

He worked as a farm boy before entering the University of Stanford where his taste for independence forces him to abandon his studies many times. Indeed, rather than classrooms, the author preferred ranches where he could better employ his energy and his freedom to read what he wanted.

Attracted by New York, he boarded a freighter in 1925, stopped for a while in Panama, and eventually reached his destination in the same year. There he did various jobs, from news reporting to building work before going back to California in 1926.

In the icy solitude of Sierra Nevada where he was in custody of a house, on the river banks of the Tahoe lake, he wrote The Golden Cup, based on memories of his stay in Panama. The editor Mac Bride accepted the manuscript and published it in 1929; by which time Steinbeck had written three novels one of which had been refused while the others had never left the author's drawers. Those three manuscripts have now been destroyed.

Married to Carol Henning in 1930, John Steinbeck ended

up leaving the house he was in custody of, and worked for a while in trout farming before settling on the Pacific coast near Carmel. He subsequently published *The Pasture of Heaven* (1932), *To a God Unknown* (1933) and finally *Tortilla Flat* (1935) that brought him out of the shadows and propelled him to the front scene. This piece of work earned him the golden medal of the Commonwealth Club of San Francisco. He actually refused to receive it in person, just as he declined the honor that was later awarded to him by his hometown by giving his name to a high school. In order to escape the publicity due to his first success, the writer fled to Mexico.

Once back home, he then published *In Dubious Battle* (1936) and *Of Mice And Men* (1937). This novel was acclaimed a perfect success by the critics and was to be one of the crowning achievements of his writing career.

The second one was to happen in 1939 when he published The Grapes of Wrath. Steinbeck judged the book too revolutionary and advised his editor to make a small print run, but the success was so great that the book was forbidden in some Californian towns. In 1940, it received the Pulitzer price when the novel was adapted for the cinema

After this success, Steinbeck continued to write even though his next novels had less impact. He divorced in 1942 and married Gwyndolyn Conger in the same year. The couple had a son in 1944 and a second one in 1946. This period was marked by several moves until the author settled again in California from 1948. He divorced once again that year and eventually met Elaine Anderson Scott in 1949 and married her in 1950. It was at that time (in 1946) that he started his research to write East of Eden that was to be published in 1949 and would bring him back to success again.

The author wrote and published several pieces of work with less impact during the following decade. A heart attack in 1959 pushed him to travel in England, Wales, and to travel around America. Those journeys led him to write and publish *The Winter of Our Discontent* in 1962 in the hope that he could get his utopian and socialist aspirations back after sinking into disillusion fifteen years earlier. The books denounced the moral decadence of America. Critics were reserved but did not prevent the book to get the Nobel Price for literature on the year of its publication.

Two years later, the author received the medal of Liberty of the United States after making another journey to Europe. From that moment, John Steinbeck was more or less absent from the literary scene and died in New York in 1968.

WORK
PRESENTATION

The Grapes of Wrath was published in 1939 by the American author John Steinbeck (1902-1968) and was awarded the Pulitzer Price the following year. The novel traces back the story of the Joads, a family of farmers from Oklahoma chased away from their land by the Bank right after the Dust Bowl, and follows their migration towards California. Unfortunately, they encounter disillusion and have to endure the obscene exploitation of the land owners who keep lowering their salaries playing on supply and demand.

This novel is a true socio-historical piece of work and Steinbeck, who thought it was too revolutionary, advised his editor to make but a small run print of it. The advice was useless, The Grapes of Wrath encountered such a great success with both the public and the critics that many Californian towns thought wise to ban it in order to prevent all kinds of social disorder.

Actually, the novels develops a strong criticism of the capitalist system, in which banks and other companies deprive people of the land which has been feeding them for many generations, leading them to misery and despair. Reduced to live with nothing, people rely on family solidarity, especially as big land owners do their best to neutralize possible unions or organization among those exploited workers.

The writer, by criticizing the function of his country, therefore develops a humanistic intention in which human beings ought to be considered above any economical aspect, above the machine and the industry and above property. Far from the common speech of the time aiming at demonizing the "reds" because of the American anxiety to see the United States be transformed into a new URSS, Steinbeck allows himself to highlight a certain vision of socialism and its necessity.

SUMMARY

I

A dust storm (the historical *Dust-Bowl*) spreads over the country and reaches Oklahoma, setting a thick layer of particules over the fields. Farmers observe the phenomenon and wonder what to do

II

A truck driver is having lunch in a small inn at the edge of the road. A man approaches the truck, waits for him to finish his lunch and asks him to take him on board to go a certain way. He says he is visiting his father whose name is Tom Joad. They talk about life, about tillers who are being driven away from their lands because they have become impossible to cultivate because of the dust. The driver asks many questions and becomes more and more ill at ease. When the vehicle reaches the junction where the passenger has to stop, the man says that he's just gotten out of jail where he was sent for murder and that he was sure the driver had realized it. Then, he gets out of the truck.

III

A tortoise moves forward by the road. It climbs the bank, with an oat straw gripped between its body and its shell. It ventures on the tarmac, ends up hit by a truck and lands on its back a few meters away. So it has spread oat seeds.

IV

Joad follows the way, and picks the tortoise up in passing in order to offer it to his younger brother. It's intensely hot

21

and the landscape is entirely covered with dust. He spots a weeping willow at the water's edge and reaches it to rest in the shadow. He meets Jim Casy, an old man he used to know when he was a child. The two men chat. Casy reveales he is no longer a clergyman since he has renounced: Joad alludes to prison, to his family. They talk about women and the meaning of life. They decide to go to Tom Joad's father's house together and eventually reach the family lands and are in view of the house.

V

It is given to see how the land owners and the bank representatives come to tell the cultivators they are being expelled from their lands because of the outstanding debts to come due to the effects of the dust storm on the upcoming harvests. They are advised to go to California. A lonely land worker, paid three dollars a day, comes on his tractor to do the work that used to be done by families of farmers and gets ready to destroy their houses.

VI

Joad and Casy stride across the ruins of their family house and where nobody is left. Joad surrenders himself to nostalgia and remember how his life used to be. He wonders if his family is dead or gone. Even the neighbourhood looks like it has been deserted. They suddenly spot a man coming in their direction. It is Muley Graves, whom the former prisoner used to know well. He explains the situation briefly: Joad's family is about to leave for California. Muley is one of the last cultivators who have stayed apart from Finley, the man who is in charge of cultivating the area with his tractor. The three men decide to have dinner on the spot and to eat the rabbits Muley has just killed. The discussion goes on. They talk particularly about the prison and the choices they have made. Casy has an epiphany. He feels that it is his duty to give a chance to those who have been expelled. A patrolling car arrives driven by Feeley. They go and hide in the cotton field before looking for a safer place to sleep.

VII

The author shows the life of a car concession through the dialogues between a boss and his employees and through the dialogues between his employees and their clients. The main goal is to force the selling in order to make the most of the emigration wave and of people looking for cars to reach California

VIII

Muley has advised Joad and Casy to leave early so as not to be caught. They walk to Joad's uncle's house where Joad's family has found shelter. The whole family is reunited and everyone is happy that Joad is back although they all ask the same question: "You didn't run away did you ?"

IX

The farmers are leaving. They sort out their belongings in order to decide what to sell and what to take away with them. They are haunted by the past and attached to those goods so they leave quickly, burning what they can't sell or take away.

X

The Joad's family has sold it's goods for almost nothing and is reunited in the evening to hold council. They are worried because Tommy is not allowed to go out of the State. They decide to allow the clergyman among them. They evaluate the situation: they will leave the following day. They kill their pigs to have food supply and load up the truck all night long. Mulay comes to say goodbye in the morning just before they leave. The grandfather no longer wants to go and so the grandmother secretly gets him drunk so he will sleep and not oppose any resistance. They eventually leave in direction of the West.

XI

The author describes workers driving tractors without bothering to know the land they are turning over. Houses are abandoned to the beasts and to the wind.

XII

Road 66 is described with its lines of vehicles going to California, with the worry that the car may break, the worries about the gossip, the rumors about the destination and the road to follow to reach it.

XIII

The truck follows the road. The family makes a stop at a service station where the owner keeps wondering where the country is going with all those people who are going away. Afterwards, they reach Oklahoma City, pass it and make a stop by the road before night fall next to a car which belongs to strangers, the Wilsons, who nevertheless accept them as neighbors. The grandfather is victim of a heart-attack when getting out of the truck and passes away on those people's mattress. The Joads bury him on the spot because of the costs of a funeral even though it is illegal. Despite the fact that he refuses to endorse the role of a clergyman, Casy gives a sermon. The two families have dinner and decide to travel together to lighten the Joads' truck in exchange for the maintenance of the Wilsons' car. The death of the grandfather makes them join the group.

XIV

This chapter is a criticism of Western landowners who are panic stricken by the emigrants' arrival and an apology for men union towards adversity and fate. It presents collective ideas as an effect and not as a cause of the problems created by property.

XV

This chapter shows various aspects of bar life on Road 66 with two employees: Al and Maé. The truck drivers are sources of joy and pay good money whilst the emigrants are a source of unease and don't have money.

XVI

The Wilsons and the Joads carry on with their journey and adapt to their new way of life. They go through Texas. The Wilsons' car suffers from a failure and a connecting rod has to be changed. After frank discussions, they choose to continue their journey and to drop the family off further on while Tom and the clergyman replace the damaged piece. Al comes back to pick his brother up with the truck. They find a car graveyard and the wanted piece while the blind employee keeps complaining about his lot until Tom reproaches him for his lack of will. They come back to the car before nightfall, mend it, and eventually get to the camp. The owner is unpleasant and wants to extort money from them. A man coming back from California who has lost everything mocks the emigrants and claims that California is a fraud where people are being exploited.

XVII

Life gets organized on the roads and people reorganize their world and reunite in the evening. They are all simultaneously nostalgic for their former life and anxious to discover their new future.

XVIII

The Wilsons and the Joads go through Arizona, Colorado before eventually reaching California. They stop their car by the river just before getting to the desert. One of the Joads' sons, Noah, decides to leave his family to stay and live by the river. He leaves while Tom keeps looking at him. A father and his son warn the Joads men that they are likely to be disappointed since the 'Okies' are not particularly welcome. Man and Rosasharn are worried about the ailing grandmother but they refuse the Jehovites to pray for her. A policeman threatens them to send them to jail if they are still in the same place the following morning. They make the decision to cross the desert that very evening. The Wilson's wife is unwell and so the two families part. The truck starts up towards the desert. Connie and Rosasharn dream about their upcoming life wishing that the others would sleep so that they could enjoy a moment of intimacy. Uncle John questions Cassy to find out if it is possible that a man can bring misfortune to other people since he believes he is responsible for all the sins he has committed. They drive safely, only being stopped at a control checkpoint. The policemen let them go thanks to the ailing grand-mother. The family reaches a green valley in the morning. They are all happy but they joy is tarnished by the grandmother's death. The mother has spent the whole night at her side but said nothing so as not to stop their journey.

XIX

Okies and migrants create a hive of activity striding across California to find work. Land owners fear the hungry crowd coming to them which could take possession of their empire if they combined their forces.

XX

The Joads pay for the burial of the grandmother and go to settle in Hooverville which is the outskirts where all the migrants are gathering. All the inhabitants of those slums are disheartened and say that there is no work. When Man makes a fricassee, a hoard of starving kids surrounds him to get some. She is so ill at ease that she can't refuse. Tom, and eventually Al, make acquaintance with Floyd. As they help him to mend his car, he hints that there may be work near Salinas, two hundred miles North. A man arrives in his car and offers work for everyone. Floyd tackles him and denounces a fraud. The sheriff steps in to subdue the dissenting man he calls "red". Floyd punches him, helped by Tom, and flees. Cassy knocks the sheriff out. A patrol arrives right after Floy's departure and the clergyman advise Tom to hide while he will turn himself in to the authorities since he has nothing to lose. Once the Police are gone, The Joads reunite. Uncle John has decided to get drunk, Connie has disappeared, and few are the ones who regret this good-for-nothing. They decide to leave. Tom goes and fetches Uncle John after visiting Floyd who is hiding with his lot. They will go North. The two men exchange farewells. Tom has to knock John out to drag him to the truck. They leave and see at a distance the burning of the shanty town by the authorities. Tom decides to go South to the governor's camp where there are no policemen with whom he could risk trouble.

XXI

The anger arises because the land owners are arming the Californian people while the hatred intensifies towards the numerous Oakies they are welcoming on purpose to lower the salaries and thus increase their margin of benefit.

XXII

The Joads arrive at the governmental camp called Weedpath at night. The watcher tells them where to settle, explains to Tom how to proceed with the central Committee that coordinates the various sections. The following morning and while everyone is still asleep, Tom has breakfast with neighbors: The Wallaces. They offer to take him with them since they might be able to find him a job. The farmer accepts but unfortunately the Western Bank forces him to lower the salary. The three men accept and the farmer warns them that a plan has been made to make trouble during the dance that is to take place the following Saturday so that the authorities have to step in and that the camp is closed. Tom spends the morning working. In the camp, Ruthie and Winfield discover with great surprise how the sanitaries work. The camp director, Jim Raw comes and visit the family. Man welcomes him with a coffee, surprised by his kindness. They are all beginning to hope again and to look like human beings once more. Man goes to the sanitaries and leaves his tent to Rosasharn in the case that the ladies committee arrives. A lady comes, makes a speech denouncing the camp's impiety and highlighting the necessity of preserving her from sin as well as her unborn baby. She is crying and has to be comforted by the camp director who is keeping an eye on this bird of ill omen. Man comes back. The committee arrives right after and makes him visit the camp. In the meantime, Ruthie tries to involve herself by force into a boawls game but she does not follow the rules. Nobody wants to play with her anymore to teach her what happens when you don't play by the rules and she runs off, crying. The men have gone to find work. Under the tent, Rosasharn tells Man she's been hired in the childcare centre. The woman who had visited them in the morning comes again and Man forces her to leave. The bird of ill omen is victim of a crisis and falls on the ground. The director advises them not to care for her since she is mad. The men come back. They have not found work.

XXIII

The Okies are looking for ways of entertaining themselves thanks to music, cinema, dance, alcohol or religion.

XXIV

On Saturday, people make the necessary arrangements for the dance. Tom is to watch over everything to prevent trouble. The whole family gets ready for the evening. The father decides to accept a job for 25 cents, thus encouraging the pauperization of migrants. Tom and his team succeed in preventing trouble and neutralize several hungry men. They are aware that difficulties are about to rise and that they will have to deal with this underlying anxiety.

XXV

Technical efforts are made to increase the production and grow new varieties of fruits. It is impossible to harvest them though and the production has to be destroyed in order to maintain the exchange rates.

XXVI

A month later, there is still no work. Man takes charge of the situation and declares it is time to move, even though it means they are going to lose to governmental camp's comfort. They decide to leave for the North the following day, where the cotton harvest is about to start. Rosasharn is about to have her baby and her mother pierces her ears while the men say goodbye to their new acquaintance. They leave early in the morning and there is much anxiety among them. Because of a flat tyre, they have to stop for the Joads to mend it. A man stops beside them and advises them to go to the Hooper's farm where they hire people to pick peaches. The families go there and discover a kind of military work camp. They are accommodated in a rudimentary shelter. They spend their day picking peaches and have to be very cautious. Man goes to the camp shop and shows the voucher corresponding to their salary to get some food. Everything is more expensive than in town and the shop belongs to the farm owners. The shop keeper acts as if he was making fun of him and of his poverty. In the evening, no one is satisfied. Tom goes on a walk to understand why there was bustle in front of the farm at their arrival. A guard explains it is because of the 'Reds' and advises him to go back to the camp. Tom obeys but follows a diverted path to leave the camp all the same. He comes face to face with Casy, the clergyman. He tells him he dicovered the power of union when he was in jail and that they are on strike against the farmers for them to increase the salaries. Policemen suddenly appear and one of them knocks Casy out with a pickaxe and kills him. Tom's anger rises. He snatches the weapon and makes him suffer the same fate as Casy before fleeing furtively to the family's shelter. In the morning, they discover Tom's injuries. His face is tumid and his nose broken. He will spend the day hiding with Rosasharn while his injuries disappear. In the evening, Winfield gets sick and they give him milk in a state of emergency since he is so badly nourished. The father evaluates the situation: the strike is over, the salaries are reduced to a half and the situation is unbearable. They have to leave quickly but unfortunately the murderer of the policeman is now being hunted. Man finds a solution and insists that Tom stay with them. They leave quickly and follow diverted roads. On the way, they encounter a sign which informs them someone is looking for people to pick cotton. Tom advises them to go and work there while he hides to let his injuries heal. They all agree to the plan.

XXVII

People work in the cotton fields and have to pay to get the bag where they put the collected cotton. They are all worrying about the upcoming winter since there is no work in that season in California.

XXVIII

People spend the day picking cotton. The Joads are happy to be sleeping in a dry wagon and have enough to eat. But one day, a fight btween children leads Ruthie to tell the other kids she has a brother who murdered someone and who has to hide. Man goes and see Tom to advise him to leave. He was expecting this situation and had kept thinking about what Casy had told him about social solidarity and wants to spread his message. When Man comes back, a man is talking to Pa: they are considering a union between Al and their daughters since they have been seeing each other for a long time. Some time later, he comes and declares he wants to marry the young girl because they are eager to leave. Rosasharn seems upset by the news but doesn't want to explain why to her mother when she questions her the following day. They spend three day in the cotton field trying to be quick since it is about to rain. Thunder rumbles on their way back to the camp and everyone gets wet.

XXIX

A storm arrives from the ocean and causes floods in the camp. There is no work anymore and people start to steal as diseases and weaknesses arise. A deleterious atmosphere spread across the country, fed into extra recruitment of sheriffs and deputies.

XXX

The men fight against the flood. Rosasharn is about to have her baby. They all spend the night fighting from every quarter. On the one side, a falling tree unfortunately destroys the flood barrier and the water rises relentlessly. On the other side, Rosasharn's baby is still born. Exhausted, the Joads eventually flee to go upright. They find a deserted barn where they encounter two men, a father and his son. The son is almost dying from hunger. Rosensharn agrees to breastfeed him since it is the only way to save him.

REASONS
OF SUCCESS

Steinbeck encounters success with The Grapes of Wrath thanks to the fact it takes place in the United States social reality of the 30's. The Great Depression that follows the 1929 economical crash, as well as the Dust Bowl, drove many people to the roads on the look out for a way to survive, and particularly the farmers and other farm workers who then massively migrated towards eastern states such as California. The revolutionary ideas displayed in the novel led the book to be forbidden in numerous towns in California in order to prevent social chaos.

Steinbeck likes to portray those precarious workers, those *paisanos* to whom he feels close to, as well as their attachment to their land. Often considered as a local writer because of this attachment to land he shares with its protagonists, Steinbeck describes the daily life of many inhabitants and incorporates those portraits in its story. This resonance to reality and to the human condition of the time is bound to move and affect the public.

Steinbeck's style is another reason for the novel's success. The simple generosity of the verb –that some will judge common- the conviction that animates the characters, the natural emotion that quietly arises from the scene: those stylistic features create an open, delicate and personal piece of poetry, which is true to the human beings appearing in the novel. Those elements subtley build the story conferring it an amplitude that goes far beyond what the story would have let believe.

Furthermore, in 1939, Steinbeck flushed out of what was slowing his stories down, tired of the criticism that had welcomed his last pieces of work. The wild romanticism of *Cup of Gold* (1929), the pantheism of *To a God Unknown* (1933), the humor of *Tortilla Flat* (1935) and libertarian belief of *In Dubious Battle* (1936) are no longer to be expected in his writing. At that time, *Of Mice And Men* (1937) was standing for the very essence of Steinbeck's work and eventually asseses its reputation while *The Grapes of Wrath* eventually stand for the crowning achievement of his career earning him the Pulitzer Price the following year thanks to the novel's adaptation for cinema.

To conclude, the success of the book owes much to its author personality since he puts a lot of himself in its story. Described as a romantic poet with high but restrained sensibility as suitable for an anglo-saxon from the first part of the XXth century, Steinbeck has become pessimistic because of his chaotic and difficult personal story, hence a strong wish for escape in his characters that invariably transforms into disillusion.

Fantasy is never far from his stories: the most atrocious pages steep into a fairytale atmosphere where the terrible stands alongside the marvelous. He depicts a cruel world, without indulgence or pity for the ordinary people who are his heroes. In this universe, the modern human being has no choice but to silently endure his condition, which explains the deep feeling of solitude emanating from Steinbeck's characters. The wandering farmers from *The Grapes of Wrath* are very representative of this aspect. Steinbeck portrays life wounded souls with much kindness towards those miserable people doomed to wander the world. The book's success owes much to his humanistic vision.

MAIN
THEMES

To begin with, *The Grapes of Wrath* tells the story of the Joads. They are farmers who have been expropriated from their lands by the bank. They are simple people who can each be described with one predominant characteristic: Tom is determined, his mother is a steady woman, Al is a womanizer, Rosasharn (for Rose of Saron) is a young pregnant woman, Ruthie and Wienfield are innocent children. These characters mainly interact in the family sphere throughout the story.

Chapter VIII [about the mother]: "*Her hazel eyes seemed to have experienced all possible tragedy and to have mounted pain and suffering like steps into a high calm and a superhuman understanding. She seemed to know, to accept, to welcome her position, the citadel of the family, the strong place that could not be taken. And since old Tom and the children could not know hurt or fear unless she acknowledged hurt and fear, she had practiced denying them in herself. And since, when a joyful thing happened, they looked to see whether joy was on her, it was her habit to build up laughter out of inadequate materials.*"

Chapter XIII: "*Al was one with his engine, every nerve listening for weaknesses, for the thumps or squeals, hums and chattering that indicate a change that may cause a breakdown. He had become the soul of the car.*"

Lands stands as the link between them all, beyond their family bonds. These people are all defined by their land, and are deeply attached to it. It contains both their family story and their personal one and provides them with food to eat since their work enables them to live. Without their land, they are nothing, and that is why it is extremely difficult for them to abandon it.

Chapter XIII: "*An' Grampa didn' die tonight. He died the minute you took 'im off the place.*"

Chapter V: "*It's our land. We measured it and broke it up. We were born on it, and we got killed on it, died on it. Even if it's no good, it's still ours. That's what makes it ours—being born on it, working it, dying on it. That makes ownership, not a paper with numbers on it.*"

Chapter IX: "*Well, take it—all junk—and give me five dollars. You're not buying only junk, [...] The bitterness we sold to the junk man—he got it all right, but we have it still. And when the owner men told us to go, that's us; and when the tractor hit the house, that's us until we're dead. To California or any place—every one a drum major leading a parade of hurts, marching with our bitterness. And some day—the armies of bitterness will all be going the same way. And they'll all walk together, and there'll be a dead terror from it.*"

Chapter VI [Muley]: "*But them sons-a-bitches at their desks, they jus' chopped folks in two for their margin a profit. They jus' cut 'em in two. Place where folks live is them folks. They ain't whole, out lonely on the road in a piled-up car. They ain't alive no more. Them sons-a-bitches killed 'em.*"

But the possession of that land, which is close to obsession, as well as finding work to survive, questions the notion of property which is the most important notion in the novel. If Steinbeck enhances property as long as it is human-sized and allow people to live properly, big land owners are described as powerful and It is therefore possible to say that Steinbeck's socialism relies on small land owners and not on collectivized lands as is the case in the Marxist ideology.

Chapter XIV: *"For the quality of owning freezes you forever into 'I,' and cuts you off forever from the 'we.'"*

Chapter XIX: *"And it came about that owners no longer worked on their farms. They farmed on paper; and they forgot the land, the smell, the feel of it, and remembered only that they owned it, remembered only what they gained and lost by it."*

Chapter XIX: *"A crop raised–why, that makes ownership. Land hoed and the carrots eaten–a man might fight for land he's taken food from. Get him off quick! He'll think he owns it. He might even die fighting for the little plot among the Jimson weeds."*

Property is therefore a cause for social illness when it is concentrated in the hands of few. From then on, landowners anxiety is the accomplishment of Marxist theories where communism replaces capitalism when the latter reaches its peak: the community would then be able to possess and fairly redistribute lands to the people who have been ruined. Since they created migrant's misery, the big land owners understandably feel threatened by those people.

Chapter XIX: *"Okies–the owners hated them because the owners knew they were soft and the Okies strong, that they were fed and the Okies hungry; and perhaps the owners had heard from their grandfathers how easy it is to steal land from a soft man if you are fierce and hungry and armed."*

Chapter XIX: *"And the great owners, who must lose their*

land in an upheaval, the great owners with access to history, with eyes to read history and to know the great fact: when property accumulates in too few hands it is taken away. And that companion fact: when a majority of the people are hungry and cold they will take by force what they need. And the little screaming fact that sounds through all history: repression works only to strengthen and knit the repressed. The great owners ignored the three cries of history."

However the threat doesn't prevent them from maintaining the absurdity of the economical system: in order to maintain the exchange rates and the prices of sale, the land owners don't hesitate to let the produce rot after having done everything in their power to produce more.

Chapter XXV: "*The little farmers watched debt creep up on them like the tide. They sprayed the trees and sold no crop, they pruned and grafted and could not pick the crop. And the men of knowledge have worked, have considered, and the fruit is rotting on the ground, and the decaying mash in the wine vat is poisoning the air.*"

Those big land owners, those firms and those banks that expropriate farmers are never named. It's like they were belonging to a great all, an unspeakable monster who devours everything in its way. Their agents, the policemen, are all reduced to embodying the machinery of a gigantic and inhuman engine that subjugates the world.

Chapter V: "'The Bank–or the Company–needs–wants–insists–must have–as though the Bank or the Company were a monster, with thought and feeling, which had ensnared them. These last would take no responsibility for the banks or the companies because they were men and slaves, while the banks were machines and masters all at the same time. »

Chapter V: "*The bank is something else than men. It happens that every man in a bank hates what the bank does, and yet the bank does it. The bank is something more than men, I tell you. It's the monster. Men made it, but they can't control it. [...] You'll be stealing if you try to stay, you'll be murderers if you kill to stay. The monster isn't men, but it can make men do what it wants.*"

The worker replacing the farmers is but a tool in the firms' hands. He is disembodied , reduced to an anonymous function into the economical system, that is to say a machine, just like the tractor he is driving. Human land working does not exist anymore: industrialization has killed the farmer, the soul and the nobility of his work, and has replaced it with something cold and impersonal.

Chapter V: "*The man sitting in the iron seat did not look like a man; gloved, goggled, rubber dust mask over nose and mouth, he was a part of the monster, a robot in the seat. [...] the monster that sent the tractor out, had somehow got into the driver's hands, into his brain and muscle, had goggled him and muzzled him–goggled his mind, muzzled his speech, goggled his perception, muzzled his protest. He could not see the land as it was, he could not smell the land as it smelled; his feet did not stamp the clods or feel the warmth and power of the earth. He sat in an iron seat and stepped on iron pedals. [...]He did not know or own or trust or beseech the land. [...]He loved the land no more than the bank loved the land. [...]No man had touched the seed, or lusted for the growth. Men ate what they had not raised, had no connection*

45

*with the bread. The land bore under iron, and under iron gra-
dually died; for it was not loved or hated, it had no prayers
or curses.* »

By playing as they do on the economic and property level,
land-owners consciously create an unfair global system to
which the population can't but be subjected.

Chapter VII: "*Get 'em under obligation. Make 'em take
up your time. Don't let 'em forget they're takin' your time.
People are nice, mostly. They hate to put you out. Make 'em
put you out, an' then sock it to.*"

Chapter X: "*And now they were weary and frightened because they had gone against a system they did not understand
and it had beaten them.*"

But that corrupt system takes its roots in human misery and
is maintained by the violence of legal authorities (policemen)
who see in this disorder a threat to social order. It's truly a
vicious circle: poor people get poorer, authorities move them
on elsewhere and they become even poorer and have to work
for even less money, and so on.

Chapter XVI: "*Why–it's like–it's like they was runnin'
away from soldiers.*"

Chapter VI [Muley]: "*If on'y they didn't tell me I got to get
off, why, I'd prob'y be in California right now a-eatin' grapes
an' a-pickin' an orange when I wanted. But them sons-a-bitches says I got to get off–an', Jesus Christ, a man can't, when
he's tol' tode !*"

Chapter XVIII [Man & a policeman]: "*We aim to get out tonight an' cross the desert, mister.*"

"*Well, you better. If you're here tomorra this time I'll run you in. We don't want none of you settlin' down here.*"

The obvious injustice doesn't lead the migrants to unite, though, since they don't know who to blame for their misfortune. The enemy is anonymous and inaccessible so that they have to leave it to themselves and to fate.

Chapter V: "*I don't aim to starve to death before I kill the man that's starving me.*"

"*I don't know. Maybe there's nobody to shoot. Maybe the thing isn't men at all.*

Maybe like you said, the property's doing it."

The most surprising – and the most perverse – element in the story is that large numbers of Okies cross the country in order to find work. They therefore possess a strong potential power that causes fear among the land-owners. However, the migrants are so exhausted by the living conditions that they have become unable to fight against the lethargy into which the loss of their lands has plunged them.

Chapter VIII: "*They say there's a hun'erd thousand of us shoved out. If we was all mad the same way, Tommy–they wouldn't hunt nobody down–*"

[…] "*Many folks feel that way?*" he demanded.

"*I don't know. They're jus' kinda stunned. Walk aroun' like they was half asleep.*"

In the end, their very number is a handicap to them since the land-owners play on supply and demand in order to lower the salaries and therefore the costs of production. The more misery they face, the more they become exploitable and profitable.

Chapter XII: "*The whole United States ain't that big. It ain't that big. It ain't big enough. There ain't room enough for you an' me, for your kind an' my kind, for rich and poor together all in one country, for thieves and honest men. For hunger and fat.*"

Chapter XX: "*We ain't no bums,*" *Tom insisted.* "*We're lookin' for work. We'll take any kind a work.*"
The young man paused in fitting the brace to the valve slot. He looked in amazement at Tom. "*Lookin' for work?*" *he said.* "*So you're lookin' for work. What ya think ever'body else is lookin' for? Di'monds? What you think I wore my ass down to a nub lookin' for?*"

Chapter XXII [a farmer]: "*There's always red agitators just before a pay cut.*"

This increasing misery ends up by reducing men and women to less than beasts in the minds of the authorities and of those of the local population. They have become a herd of animals that have to be gathered together, and dealt with in order to shear them better.

Chapter XVIII [an anonymous man at the service station]: "*Well, you and me got sense. Them goddamn Okies got no sense and no feeling. They ain't human. A human being wouldn't live like they do. A human being couldn't stand it to be so dirty and miserable. They ain't a hell of a lot better than gorillas.*"

Chapter XVIII [Man]: "*I pray God we gonna be let to wash some clothes. We ain't never been dirty like this. Don't even wash potatoes 'fore we boil 'em. I wonder why? Seems like the heart's took out of us.*'"

Chapter XXIX: "*Fella had a team of horses, had to use 'em to plow an' cultivate an' mow, wouldn' think a turnin' 'em out to starve when they wasn't workin'. Them's horses–we're men.*"

They end up by being disillusioned: Steinbeck is used to creating characters who fight to make their dreams come true. Even though they fail they keep fighting for their broken dreams. The green Eden the big land=owners promised becomes instead a purgatory for exploited people, a waiting room for hell where you can hear the cries of these miserable creatures.

Chapter XVIII: "*"Well, we're here. This here's California, an' she don't look so prosperous." [...]Never seen such tough mountains. This here's a murder country. This here's the bones of a country. Wonder if we'll ever get in a place where folks can live 'thout fightin' hard scrabble an' rocks.*'"

However, migrants continue to hope, even in adversity, which helps them and gives them the strength to continue their journey. The Joads see nobility in their condition, a kind of eternity for the people who hold tighter every day to their precious belongings.

Chapter I: "*The men were silent and they did not move often. And the women came out of the houses to stand beside their men–to feel whether this time the men would break. The women studied the men's faces secretly, for the corn could go, as long as something else remained. [...]Women and children knew deep in themselves that no misfortune was too great to bear if their men were whole."*

Chapter XX [Man and Tom]: *"Why, Tom–us people will go on livin' when all them people is gone. Why, Tom, we're the people that live. They ain't gonna wipe us out. Why, we're the people–we go on."*

"We take a beatin' all the time."

"I know." Ma chuckled. "Maybe that makes us tough. Rich fellas come up an' they die, an' their kids ain't no good, an' they die out. But, Tom, we keep a-comin'. Don' you fret none, Tom. A different time's comin'."

Chapter XXVI [Man]: *"If you're in trouble or hurt or need–go to poor people. They're the only ones that'll help– the only ones."*

Chapter XXIX: *"[...] the break had not come; and the break would never come as long as fear could turn to wrath."*

People live in the hope of a better future for themselves and for their families. They often talk about correspondence courses, especially Connie before he runs away.

Chapter I [Tom and the truck dirver]: *"I don't never take a drink till I'm through."*

"Yeah?" Joad asked.

"Yeah! A guy got to get ahead. Why, I'm thinkin' of takin' one of them correspondence school courses. Mechanical engineering. It's easy. Just study a few easy lessons at home. I'm

thinkin' of it. Then I won't drive no truck. Then I'll tell other guys to drive trucks."

In particular, migrants are capable of organizing them-selves thanks to their hopes for a better future. Self-manage-ment (which is a recurring theme among the Transcendenta-lists and the Libertarians) is often mentioned as the best way of breaking loose from obligations and pressure created by the system created by the land-owners. Unfortunately, the Okies can't unite and work together and these initiatives can't spread despite the fact that those that do exist have a really positive impact. Time and again, migrants discover existing initiatives and go from one place to another instead of crea-ting something of their own.

Chapter XVII: *"Every night a world created, complete with furniture–friends made and enemies established; a world complete with braggarts and with cowards, with quiet men, with humble men, with kindly men. Every night relationships that make a world, established; and every morning the world torn down like a circus."*

Chapter XXII [Thomas Wallace]: *"Those folks in the camp are getting used to being treated like humans. When they go back to the squatters' camps they'll be hard to handle."*

Chapter XXII [Timothy Wallace]: *"People there look out for theirselves. Got the nicest strang band in these parts. [...] I guess the big farmers is scairt of that. Can't throw us in jail– why, it scares 'em. Figger maybe if we can gove'n ourselves, maybe we'll do other things."*

The idea of Civil obedience is dear to Thoreau (if a law

is unfair, then you have to disobey it) and it is another trans-cendentalist element that is very important in the novel. If migrants can't really manage themselves, they nevertheless dare to overstep the boundaries of legality in order to do what has to be done in the name of moral duty.

Chapter XIII: "*Sometimes the law can't be foller'd no way,*" *said Pa.* "*Not in decency, anyways. They's lots a times you can't. [...] Et je maintiens que j'ai le droit d'enterrer mon propre père. [...]. I'm sayin' now I got the right to bury my own pa.*"
"*Law changes,*" *he said [the clergyman],* "*but 'got to's' go on. You got the right to do what you got to do.*"

When this happens, it is surprising that, amongst those who disobey, none dare to deny their social status. Instead, all claim it with pride. The explanation may lie in a generally ac-cepted feature of American culture, the Judeo-Christian rela-tionship to suffering and misery: man is meant to endure and toil, to earn his bread by the sweat of his brow during his time on earth. Therefore, it is normal that the Okie masses suffer in silence. Moreover, the concept of sin comes up frequently in the novel, which asks deep questions about the values of the society about which Steinbeck writes.

Chapter IV [Casy]: "*There ain't no sin and there ain't no virtue. There's just stuff people do. It's all part of the same thing. And some of the things folks do is nice, and some ain't nice, but that's as far as any man got a right to say.*'" *[...] Maybe,' I figgered, 'maybe it's all men an' all women we love; maybe that's the Holy Sperit–the human sperit–the whole she-bang. Maybe all men got one big soul ever'body's a part of.*'"

Chapter VIII [Casy]: "*I got thinkin' how we was holy when we was one thing, an' mankin' was holy when it was one thing. An' it on'y got unholy when one mis'able little fella got the bit in his teeth an' run off his own way, kickin' an' draggin' an' fightin'. Fella like that bust the holiness. But when they're all workin' together, not one fella for another fella, but one fella kind of harnessed to the whole shebang–that's right, that's holy.*"

Chapter XVIII [Casy]: "*Well,*" *said Casy,* "*for anybody else it was a mistake, but if you think it was a sin–then it's a sin. A fella builds his own sins right up from the groun'.*"

Chapter XIV: "*And this you can know–fear the time when Manself will not suffer and die for a concept, for this one quality is the foundation of Manself, and this one quality is man, distinctive in the universe.*"

Another recurring question throughout the novel is about the meaning of events : the absurdity of the system created by the land owners, the meaning of life, etc. The migrants feel very confused about all these questions. Casy, the clergyman, is the one who voices them the most clearly and who eventually manages to find some answers even though they remain very unsatisfactory and even though they lead him to be killed by the authorities. It's difficult to survive in a meaningless world when human actions make it look even more absurd, this is why Tom will end up following his path in order to change things.

Chapter IV: [Casy] "*I got the call to lead people, an' no place to lead 'em.*"
"*Lead 'em around and around,*" *said Joad.* "*Sling 'em in*

the irrigation ditch. Tell 'em they'll burn in hell if they don't think like you. What the hell you want to lead 'em someplace for? Jus' lead 'em."

Chapter XIII [Casy]: "I been walkin' aroun' in the country. Ever'body's askin' that. What we comin' to? Seems to me we don't never come to nothin'. Always on the way. Always goin' and goin'. Why don't folks think about that? They's movement now. People moving. We know why, an' we know how. Movin' 'cause they got to. That's why folks always move. Movin' 'cause they want somepin better 'n what they got. An' that's the on'y way they'll ever git it. Wantin' it an' needin' it, they'll go out an' git it. It's bein' hurt that makes folks mad to fightin'."

Chapter XXVI: "If a fella owns a team a horses, he don't raise no hell if he got to feed 'em when they ain't workin'. But if a fella got men workin' for him, he jus' don't give a damn. Horses is a hell of a lot more worth than men. I don' understan' it."

In the end, the feeling that arises from *The Grapes of Wrath* is a feeling of permanent headlong rush, as if it were the only valid solution, expressing all the greatness of man and the solidarity.

Chapter XII: "66 is the mother road, the road of flight."

Chapter XII: "Le's go on till she blows."

Steinbeck is a Humanist who is fascinated by his companion in misery in this world and therefore makes an apology for the will to survive despite all adversity. He also suggests in his novel that the system and powerful people get what they spread in people's hearts and have to take the responsibilties for their sinful actions.

Chapter VI [Casy]: "*They got to live before they can afford to die.*"

Chapter XXV: "In the souls of the people the grapes of wrath are filling and growing heavy, growing heavy for the vintage."

ANALYSIS OF THE
LITERARY MOVEMENT

As an author, John Steinbeck, is placed at the parting of the ways, between American transcendentalism and European realism. He drew from these two traditions and works to create a social story deeply rooted in a local and historical framework in each of his books. Because of that particular feature, he was often considered as a Californian local writer even though his novels have more depth and describe a country in which the American dream brings disillusion.

The transcendentalist movement appeared with the creation of the *Transcendental Club* by R. W. Emerson, G. Putnam and F.H. Hedge in 1836 in Chicago, New England. They were famous intellectuals and stood against the Unitarian Church and the movement led by Harvard members. They aimed at a philosophy based both on the mental and spiritual essence of the being and drew their inspiration mainly from Kant and from German idealism. The influence of the movement created by the English romantics and that of the Oriental philosophy led some people to think of that movement as late American romanticism. The transcendentalists aim to revolutionize the mind and humanity by promoting the respect for all living beings and wonder towards nature and the environment.

The publishing of *Nature* in 1836 by R.W. Emerson signalled the birth of the movement and the beginning of its existence on the literary scene. H. D. Thoreau, author of *Civil Disobedience* was considered to be one of the major authors of the movement with his novel *Walden, or Life in the woods* (1854) inspired by his own personal experience. These two books are regarded as the two major pieces of work of the movement and unfortunately eclipse the others.

From that time, transcendentalism continued to influence American literature by emphasizing the importance of nature in the story but without being considered as a major movement in the American literary scene. That influence is still visible nowadays through nature writing with authors such as C. Johnson or D. Vann.

Realism appeared in the second part of the nineteenth century as a reaction against romanticism, which was coming to an end. Realism aims to be a way of fighting against sentimentalism and against the Romantics. By stripping novels of idealism and literary artifice, realistic authors can write about popular subjects such as working conditions, social unrest, marital relationships, etc. Those themes are also exploited by the Naturalists but in a rather different way. They aim to describe reality as it is and to be faithful to what exists in total liberty.

In France, the movement rose with authors such as Stendhal, Balzac, and, more particularly, with Flaubert and his novel *Madame Bovary* (1857). Thanks to translations, Realism reached Europe and Great Britain. A while later, Scandinavian dramatists appropriated the movement in order to bring more reality to theatre and found success in this.

The movement finally declined in the 1890's but nevertheless existed until 1960 thanks to its late export to the United States a few decades later. It also reached the USSR in an alternative version known as social realism, which was the only literary movement authorized under the regime. Nevertheless, the movement still influences writers nowadays, more particularly thanks to its determination to describe reality authentically in all its vulgarity and splendor.